dinner.

James McIntosh

www.jamesmcintosh.co.uk

word4word

dinner.

© James McIntosh.
ISBN: 978-1-906316-19-8.
All rights reserved. No part of this publication may be reproduced, stored in
a retrieval system, or transmitted in any form, or by any means, electronic,
mechanical, photocopying, recording or otherwise, without the prior
permission of the publisher.
A copy of this publication has been registered with the British Library.
Published by Word4Word in 2009.
8 King Charles Court, Evesham, Worcestershire WR11 4RF.
www.w4wdp.com.
Printed in the UK by TJ International .
Photography by Ash Photography Ltd.

Designed and typeset by www.jellygraphics.co.uk

Have dinner with James

Believe me, I do understand what it's like to come home from work tired, wondering what to cook for dinner. The day has been busy, a thousand things are running through your head and all you want to do is sit down, switch off, relax and have a quiet evening. Is home ever like that? Not mine! I mean, I don't have kids to feed, but I generally have preparation to do for the next day for work, mates calling around for something to eat, shirts to iron, and the list goes on…

So, back to what's going through your head on the journey home. What's to cook? What's in the fridge? What can I do with two eggs and a stem of broccoli? Oh, there is a bit of lamb in the fridge from the Sunday roast. If only I had taken those chicken breasts out of the freezer this morning. Or, perhaps it's a simple as 'I don't know what to cook!' If this sounds familiar to you, let me stress one fact. You're 'normal'!

As a Home Economist, I teach people how to cook and how to use domestic appliances to the best of their ability. Do you remember Home Economics in school? Well as a profession it's about a lot more than making buns and cakes. It's about how to cook for a family on an everyday budget. It's about how to prepare food with little or no waste. It's also about producing good home-cooked food that's not complicated to make. No fiddle, no fuss, just food.

dinner. is the second book in a series of four. Here I give you solutions to every day family meals that don't cost the earth to produce. So, in this little book I will take you through 50 meal solutions, showing you how to modify each one, giving you over 120 recipes.

So, enjoy dinner with me! You can find links to my YouTube and Facebook pages as well as featured recipes and lots more at www.jamesmcintosh.co.uk

All of James's recipes are tested five times.

P.S. The next book in the series is called *veg*.

Aperitif

There is a growing interest in saving money on ever-increasing food bills by preparing good, nutritious food at home.

With rising prices of fuel as well as food, it's important to think conservation when cooking. As few pots and pans as possible are suggested so that you save fuel and can cook with as little washing up as possible.

There is a great debate over what exactly British cuisine is. *dinner.* contains food from all over the world to reflect the diversity of the modern-day British household.

dinner. is small enough to keep in your handbag, manbag or pocket (so you have a readymade shopping list when shopping) yet comprehensive enough to feed the family. All recipes in this book will feed four people. If there are less than four to feed, why not freeze left over portions for use later? This is an essential cookery book for young people who want to learn how to make great everyday meals, for families interested in saving money on food bills and for teachers and students of Home Economics/Food Technology.

Contents

	Ten ways to save money when cooking at home	page	8
1	turkish kebabs.	page	10
2	pork spare ribs.	page	12
3	lemon garlic chicken.	page	13
4	stir-fry chicken with bok choi.	page	14
5	asian chicken and spinach curry.	page	16
6	pork schnitzel.	page	18
7	mushroom stroganoff.	page	20
8	baked honey pork fillets.	page	22
9	pork with mustard and apple.	page	24
10	beef olives with thyme and juniper.	page	26
11	irish stew.	page	28
12	chicken with lemon wedges and thyme.	page	30
13	moroccan lamb and couscous.	page	32
14	lasagne with a ton of basil.	page	34
15	chilli con carne.	page	36
16	moussaka.	page	38
17	chicken and mushroom pie.	page	40
18	steak and ale pie.	page	42
19	chicken fajitas.	page	43
20	tagliatelle and meat balls.	page	44
21	devilled chicken supremes.	page	45
22	prawn, orange and ginger stir-fry.	page	46
23	coq au vin.	page	47
24	simple fish pie.	page	48
25	chicken á la king.	page	49

26	pancetta, pork and pea risotto.	page **50**
27	venison casserole.	page **52**
28	stuffed bacon rolls.	page **54**
29	chicken casserole.	page **55**
30	spaghetti carbonara.	page **56**
31	beef curry.	page **57**
32	braised lamb shanks in red wine and balsamic.	page **58**
33	sweet and sour pork.	page **60**
34	kedgeree.	page **62**
35	penne arrabiata.	page **64**
36	sole florentine.	page **65**
37	jambalaya.	page **66**
38	bœuf bourguignon.	page **68**
39	teriyaki beef stir-fry.	page **70**
40	carbonade de bœuf.	page **72**
41	coley and lemongrass with a parsley sauce.	page **73**
42	rich braised beef with herb dumplings.	page **74**
43	thai chicken curry.	page **76**
44	beef goulash.	page **78**
45	steak and kidney pie.	page **80**
46	paella.	page **82**
47	chinese lamb chops.	page **84**
48	macaroni cheese.	page **85**
49	lancashire hotpot.	page **86**
50	chicken tagine.	page **88**
	index of recipes.	page **91**

Ten ways to save money when cooking at home

1 Never shop when you're hungry – you will only buy things you don't need. Always have a shopping list – it's best to plan a week's meals before shopping, eliminating from your list what you already have in your cupboard.

2 Use cast iron when cooking – you will cut your fuel bills. Cast iron loves heat, it gets hot quickly and you can lower temperatures. So, for example, you can cook on a medium heat on the hob rather than a roaring flame. Likewise, when using cast iron there will be enough residual heat in the dish and in the oven 10 minutes before the end of cooking, so you can turn the oven off. Always ensure food is piping hot before serving.

3 Fruit is as filling as a lot of chocolates and crisps, and it's cheaper too when it's in season. And think of all the calories you are saving!

4 Freeze left-over portions. Give children smaller portions, they can always have more but there'll be less waste on the plate if they don't eat it all.

5 Keep a pantry well stocked with groceries, such as herbs and spices, balsamic vinegar and stock cubes.

These all add flavour to your cooking and allow you to get the most out of cheaper cuts of meat, etc.

6 Frozen foods are generally cheaper than their fresh counterparts. Use your freezer wisely and it will save you money.

7 Use a steamer to cook fish and vegetables. If you use the stacking kind of steamer, you only need one pan. Make sure you put denser foods like potatoes on the bottom and lighter foods like greens and fish towards the top.

8 Buy fresh produce from markets and local producers. The fruit and vegetables may need a wash before use, but this does not take long. Think of all the packaging you won't be wasting!

9 Batch cook. Watch out for supermarket offers for meat. Make two batches of a recipe instead of one and freeze the other.

10 Always use a pan that's the correct size for what you're cooking. A taller pan will take longer to boil than a smaller one, so you'll use more energy, which will cost you more money.

turkish kebabs.

This is my re-creation of kebabs from a street vendor in Istanbul.

300g rump steak, cut
into 2cm cubes
4 tbsp light soy sauce
Freshly ground black pepper
1 clove garlic, crushed

1 green pepper, core removed
and cut into 2cm squares
12 shallots, peeled
12 small button mushrooms
12 cherry tomatoes
A little vegetable oil

Here's how to make it...

⚜ Mix the meat, soy sauce, pepper and garlic in a glass dish, cover and place into the fridge for an hour to marinate.

⚜ Place 8 wooden skewers in cold water for about an hour.

⚜ Preheat the grill to a high heat.

⚜ Evenly arrange the meat, peppers, shallots, mushrooms and tomatoes onto skewers. Brush with oil.

⚜ Grill for 10–15 minutes, turning frequently.

⚜ **2, 3 and 4 Oven Aga,** cook on the 1st set of runners in the Roasting Oven for 10–15 minutes.

⚜ **Rayburn,** cook on the 1st set of runners in the Main Oven with the Thermodial reading Roast for 10–15 minutes.

Serve with... Freshly cooked white or pilaf rice.

Variations

Chinese five spice chicken kebabs *Replace the beef with chicken and add 1 tbsp Chinese five spice to the marinade.*

Greek souvlaki kebabs *Replace the beef with lamb and replace the soy sauce with 1 tbsp mint jelly.*

Satay kebabs *Coat beef with smooth peanut butter instead of soy sauce.*

James says...

Soaking the wooden skewers before using prevents them from burning and splintering during cooking. Although it makes cleaning up easier, never put kitchen foil under a grill pan as this can reflect the heat back up towards the elements and damage them.

pork spare ribs.

I don't know about you, but I love to pick around the bone when eating ribs. Gooey fingers!

600g pork ribs
2 tbsp black bean or hoisin sauce

Here's how to make it...

- Coat the ribs in the sauce, place into a dish and cover. Refrigerate for 1 hour.
- Preheat the grill to a high heat.
- Grill for 10–15 minutes, turning frequently.
- **2, 3 and 4 Oven Aga,** cook on the 1st set of runners in the Roasting Oven for 10–15 minutes.
- **Rayburn,** cook on the 1st set of runners in the Main Oven with the Thermodial reading Roast for 10–15 minutes.

Serve with... Potato, parsnip and butternut squash chips.

Variations

Honey and sesame seed spare ribs *Replace the black bean sauce with runny honey and mix through 2 tbsp sesame seeds.*

Spicy marmalade spare ribs *Replace the black bean sauce with thick cut marmalade and 1–2 chillies finely chopped.*

Curry spare ribs *Replace black bean sauce with curry paste.*

James says...

Ribs can be coated in the marinade and frozen until needed. To defrost, just remove from freezer and leave in the fridge overnight.

lemon garlic chicken.

A quick and easy supper with a great deal of flavour.

600g boned chicken
pieces, skinned and cut
into bite-sized pieces
2 tbsp plain flour
1 tsp paprika or
cayenne pepper

Sauce
1 tbsp hoisin sauce
Finely grated zest and
juice of 2 lemons
1 garlic clove, crushed

Here's how to make it...

- Preheat oven to 180°C (160°C if using a fan oven) or Gas Mark 4.
- Toss chicken in flour and paprika or cayenne and set into a baking dish in a single layer. Bake for 15 minutes.
- Combine all sauce ingredients, pour over chicken and cook for a further 15 minutes until tender.
- **2, 3 and 4 Oven Aga**, cook on the 4th set of runners in the Roasting Oven.
- **Rayburn**, cook on the 4th set of runners in the Main Oven with the Thermodial reading Roast.

Serve with... Roast potatoes and seasonal green vegetables.

Variations

Orange garlic chicken *Replace lemon with orange.*

James says...

Hoisin sauce is made from soy bean paste with garlic, sugar and chillies.

stir-fry chicken with bok choi.

Stir-fries are quick to cook. It may look like
there are lots of vegetables to prepare, but
don't fret – you only need quarter the bok choi
as they come apart when being stir-fried.

*400g chicken strips
or diced chicken
2 tbsp dry sherry
1 tbsp light soy sauce
4 bok choi, cut into 4 lengthways
1 tbsp nut oil
½ onion, diced
1 clove garlic, crushed*

*1 tsp freshly grated ginger
2 spring onions, sliced diagonally
250ml water
2 tsp cornflour
1 x 400g can baby corn, drained
1 small chilli, seeded and
finely diced (optional)*

Here's how to make it...

- Mix chicken, sherry and soy sauce. Cover and set aside.
- Bring a pan of water to the boil and add bok choy. After 1 minute drain and set aside.
- Heat oil in wok, add onion, garlic, ginger and spring onions. Stir-fry for 30 seconds until fragrant. Add chicken and stir-fry for 2 minutes.
- Mix water and cornflour until smooth, add to wok and bring to the boil. Add corn and chilli (if using) and simmer for 10 minutes.
- Place bok choi on a plate with the chicken on top.
- **2, 3 and 4 Oven Aga,** heat wok and stir-fry on the Boiling Plate.
- **Rayburn,** heat wok and stir-fry on the hot end of the hotplate.

Serve with...
Rice or cellophane noodles cooked in the water drained from the bok choi.

Variations
Stir-fry pork and bok choi *Replace chicken with pork.*

Stir-fry beef and bok choi *Replace chicken with beef.*

James says...
Choose a wok wisely. Hard anodised woks heat up the quickest and the sides will heat too. Stainless steel is a poor conductor of heat and takes a long time to come up to temperature. It's important to have the wok really hot before starting to cook.

asian chicken and spinach curry.

Greens and protein all in one!

1 tbsp vegetable oil
4 chicken thighs, skinned
½ onion, chopped
1 tsp freshly grated ginger
2 tbsp curry paste
2 cloves garlic, crushed

1 x 125g can chopped tomatoes
100g button mushrooms
100g spinach leaves, washed
150g fresh or dried noodles
1 tsp chilli paste, or
½ chilli chopped

Here's how to make it...

- Heat the oil in a casserole dish, add the chicken thighs and cook on the hob for about 15 minutes.
- Add onion, ginger, curry paste and garlic and cook for another 5 minutes.
- Add tomatoes and mushrooms, cook for a further 15 minutes.
- Bring a pan of water to the boil.
- Stir spinach leaves into mixture, reduce heat and allow to wilt.
- Place noodles into pan of boiling water and cook until soft, drain.
- Stir chilli through noodles and arrange noodles on plates. Place chicken and sauce on top of noodles.
- **2, 3 and 4 Oven Aga,** cook on the 4th set of runners of the Roasting Oven instead of the hob.
- **Rayburn,** either cook on the 4th set of runners of the Main Oven with the Thermodial reading Roast or the hot end of the hotplate.

Serve with... Nothing, just on its own.

Variations

Asian chicken and watercress curry *Replace spinach with watercress.*

Asian almond chicken and spinach curry *Add 2 tbsp sliced almonds to chicken when adding spinach.*

James says...

Cooking in a cast iron casserole dish means a medium heat can be used as cast iron absorbs heat so a lower heat setting will produce good results. A stainless steel dish will require a higher heat.

pork schnitzel.

Originally from Vienna, schnitzel is traditionally made with veal. For ethical as well as economic reasons I like to do this recipe with pork.

4 pork chops
Freshly squeezed juice of 1 lemon
2 tbsp plain flour
Salt and freshly ground
black pepper

1 egg, beaten
1 tbsp milk
100g fresh breadcrumbs
40g butter
2 tbsp vegetable oil

Here's how to make it...

- Remove the meat from the bone and using a meat mallet, beat the chops gently until they are about half their original thickness. Place into a non-metallic dish and pour lemon juice over them. Cover and place into the fridge for 1 hour turning the meat twice.

- Mix the flour with salt and pepper and use to evenly cover the pork.

- Mix the egg and milk together and dip the floured meat first into this mixture and then into the breadcrumbs. Press firmly to ensure the breadcrumbs stick.

- Heat butter and oil in a heavy-based frying pan and fry for 3 minutes on each side. Drain onto absorbent kitchen paper.

- **2, 3 and 4 Oven Aga,** cook on the floor of the Roasting Oven for 7–10 minutes turning once.

- **Rayburn,** cook on the hot end of the hotplate with the Thermodial on a rising heat between Bake and Roast.

Serve with... German spätzle, which are buttered noodles.

Variations

Chicken schnitzel *Replace pork with chicken breasts.*

Turkey schnitzel *Replace pork with turkey breast slices.*

James says...

It's important to beat the meat using a meat mallet to tenderise the cuts and make them thinner so they cook quicker. The lemon juice also helps to tenderise as well as flavour the meat.

mushroom stroganoff.

Not every meal needs to be meat based. I'm not vegetarian, I like my meat too much, but the texture of the mushrooms gives this recipe a good bite.

2 tbsp vegetable oil
1 onion, finely chopped
350g mixed mushrooms, eg oyster, shitake, button and chestnut, cut into large pieces
50ml red wine

2 tbsp sour cream
1 tbsp tomato puree
1 tsp Dijon mustard
Salt and freshly ground black pepper

Here's how to make it...

- Using a large frying or sauté pan, heat the pan on a medium setting, add the oil and heat for a moment.
- Add onion and sauté gently until softened but not coloured.
- Add all the mushrooms and cook for about 5 minutes until beginning to soften.
- Stir through all other ingredients, cook for a further 2–3 minutes and stir to a smooth consistency.
- **2, 3 and 4 Oven Aga**, cook on the floor of the Roasting Oven.
- **Rayburn**, cook on the floor of the Main Oven with the Thermodial reading Roast.

Serve with... Plain or brown boiled rice.

Variations

Chicken stroganoff *Replace mushrooms with 350g diced chicken breasts. Cook chicken for 10 minutes before adding wine and other ingredients.*

Pork stroganoff *Replace mushrooms with 350g diced pork. Cook pork for 10 minutes before adding wine and other ingredients.*

Beef stroganoff *Replace mushrooms with 350g diced beef. Cook beef for 10 minutes before adding wine and other ingredients.*

Turkey stroganoff *Replace mushrooms with 350g diced turkey. Cook turkey for 10 minutes before adding wine and other ingredients.*

James says...

Only one pan to wash up. Fantastic! No need to spend a lot on the wine. Use the cheap red cooking wine available in supermarkets.

baked honey pork fillets.

The sherry is optional in this recipe. But go on, why not put it in? And have a glass yourself! Cook's perks!

1 tbsp tomato puree
2 tbsp runny honey
2 tsp light soy sauce
400g pork fillets

Sauce
125ml chicken stock
1 tbsp dry sherry
2 tsp runny honey
1 tsp light soy or oyster sauce

Here's how to make it...

- Combine tomato puree, honey and soy sauce to make marinade in a baking dish. Add pork fillets, mix through to coat, cover and refrigerate for at least 1 hour.
- Preheat oven to 200°C (180°C if using a fan oven) or Gas Mark 6.
- Remove pork from refrigerator and drain off excess marinade into a small saucepan. Bake for 25 minutes.
- Place sauce ingredients into a saucepan and cook over a low heat stirring continuously for about 3 minutes.
- Cut pork into slices and serve with sauce over the top.
- **2, 3 and 4 Oven Aga,** cook pork on the 4th set of runners in the Roasting Oven for 25 minutes.
- **Rayburn,** cook on the 4th set of runners in the Main Oven with the Thermodial reading Roast for 25 minutes.

Serve with...Vegetable stir-fry or plain boiled rice.

Variations

Baked honey chicken fillets *Replace pork with chicken.*

Baked honey butternut squash *Replace pork with large slices of peeled butternut squash.*

James says...

Marinating is a great way to add flavour to meat and tenderise it at the same time. Why not prepare this the night before and leave to marinate in the fridge overnight?

pork with mustard and apple.

Really, really quick to make and it's also a good meal for a romantic night for two. Well, it worked for me!

1 small onion
5 cloves
300ml milk
1 tbsp vegetable oil
1 tbsp butter
4 pork chops or loins
1 dessert apple, cored and sliced

Mustard sauce
15g plain flour
15g butter
1 tsp English mustard
1 tsp wholegrain mustard
Salt and freshly ground black pepper

Here's how to make it...

◎ Cut top and bottom off onion and peel off skin. Push the cloves into the side of the onion. Place in a small saucepan with the milk and bring to the boil. Turn off heat and leave to one side.

◎ Heat the oil and butter in a large frying pan and fry the pork chops for 15–20 minutes. Five minutes before the end of the cooking time, tip in the apple slices and fry these with the pork, turning to brown evenly.

◎ While the pork is cooking make the mustard sauce. Remove the cloves and onion with a slotted spoon, along with any skin on the surface of the milk. Turn on the heat, add the flour and butter and whisk while bringing up to the boil. Spoon in the mustards and season well. Cook for a further 2–3 minutes.

◎ Serve pork chops with mustard sauce poured over, and top with the slices of fried apple.

Serve with... New potatoes and steamed green vegetables.

James says...

A heavy-based pan will conduct heat much better than one with a thinner base. This saves fuel when cooking.

beef olives with thyme and juniper.

Great comfort food on a cold evening.

4 thin slices rump steak
25g butter
1 onion, finely chopped
225g mushrooms, chopped
50g plain white rice
150ml water
2 tbsp fresh thyme chopped
or 1 tbsp dried thyme

6 juniper berries, crushed
Salt and freshly ground
black pepper
1 tbsp vegetable oil
25g butter
2 tbsp plain flour
125ml beef stock
1 x 200g tin chopped tomatoes

Here's how to make it...

- Preheat oven to 180°C (160°C if using a fan oven) or Gas Mark 4.
- Thump meat with mallet to tenderise.
- Melt butter in a small pan, add onion, mushrooms, rice and water.
- Bring to the boil, reduce heat and simmer for 10 minutes.
- Remove from the heat and add herbs, juniper and seasoning.
- Divide mixture and place in the middle of the beef slices, roll up and tie with string or use a cocktail stick to secure.
- Place oil into a casserole dish and heat on the hob, add the beef olives and brown on all sides. Remove from pan and set aside.
- Melt butter in casserole, add flour and cook through for a few moments until sandy in colour. Add stock and stir through. When combined add tomatoes. Stir. Return beef olives to casserole and place into oven for 1½ hours until tender.

- 🍸 **2, 3 and 4 Oven Aga,** cook casserole in the Simmering Oven for 1 ½ hours.
- 🍸 **Rayburn,** cook on the 4th set of runners in the Main Oven with the Thermodial reading Simmer or in the Lower Oven with the Thermodial reading Roast.

Serve with... A good buttery mash and braised cabbage.

Variations

Beef olives with parsley and breadcrumbs *Replace thyme with freshly chopped parsley and replace rice with fresh bread crumbs. Omit the water.*

James says...

Juniper is key in flavouring gin. Mother's ruin. Mine too. Juniper is responsible for gin's name, which is a shortening of the Dutch word for juniper, genever.

irish stew.

Traditionally made without carrots, I grew up on this stuff. I love it. In Northern Irish we have a great term: 'Get tore in!'. It means, eat and enjoy!

2 tsp vegetable oil
1 onion, diced
500g diced lamb
2 carrots, peeled and thickly sliced

6 large potatoes, peeled and thickly sliced
450ml lamb or vegetable stock made with 2 stock cubes

Here's how to make it...

- Place a large saucepan with a heavy base onto the hob and add oil. Heat through for a few moments, add onion and sauté until soft but without colour.
- Add lamb and seal on all sides for a few moments.
- Add carrots, potatoes and stock. Bring to the boil, cover and simmer gently for 30 minutes until cooked.
- **2, 3 and 4 Oven Aga**, cook in the Simmering Oven.
- **Rayburn,** cook on the 4th set of runners in the Main Oven with the Thermodial reading Simmer or in the Lower Oven with the Thermodial reading Roast.

Serve with...Nothing! Just great on its own!

Variations

Herb Irish stew *Add 1 tbsp freshly chopped thyme or 1 tsp dried thyme.*

James says...

Irish stew can be made with lamb chops as well as diced lamb. By using chops, more lamb flavour from the bones will permeate into the finished dish.

chicken with lemon wedges and thyme.

Some friends were having a party and I was volunteered to cook! This recipe is not expensive to make.

1 tbsp vegetable oil
10g butter
12 chicken drumsticks
or 8 chicken thighs

2 red onions, quartered
2 lemons, quartered
1 bunch fresh thyme

Here's how to make it...

- Preheat oven to 200°C (180°C if using a fan oven) or Gas Mark 7.
- Place a roasting tray on the hob and heat the oil and butter. Add the chicken and brown all over until crispy.
- Add onions and squeeze the lemon over the chicken. Place the lemon quarters and thyme on top and place into the oven for 45 minutes. Discard thyme and lemon before serving.
- **2, 3 and 4 Oven Aga,** cook on the 4th set of runners in the Roasting Oven for 45 minutes.
- **Rayburn,** cook on the 4th set of runners in the Main Oven with the Thermodial reading Roast for 45 minutes.

Serve with... Spicy potato wedges.

Variations

Sticky chicken with lemon wedges and thyme *Add 4 tbsp runny honey to chicken before adding lemon juice.*

James says...

Not only does this make a low cost dinner, it's also great for buffets and parties.

moroccan lamb and couscous.

I've been to Morocco – an interesting place.
The food is fantastic there; the hygiene
minimal; the alcohol, non existent!

500g lamb steak, cut
into bite sized pieces

Marinade

4 cloves garlic, finely chopped
1 tbsp fresh oregano, chopped
1 tbsp dry sherry
1 tsp fresh ginger, chopped
2 tbsp olive oil
1 tsp brown sugar
1 tsp cinnamon
Salt and freshly ground
black pepper

Couscous

225g couscous
2 tsp ground coriander
1 tsp paprika
1 tsp cumin
1 tsp turmeric
1 tsp cinnamon
1 x 400g can chick peas, drained
75g ready to eat
apricots, chopped
300ml vegetable stock, boiling

Here's how to make it...

◎ Preheat oven to 220°C (200°C if using a fan oven) or Gas Mark 7.

◎ Place the lamb into a glass or ceramic dish and add all of the marinade
  ingredients. Mix to combine. Cover and place in the refrigerator for at
  least 1 hour.

◎ Pour into a casserole dish and brown the meat on the hob. Cover and
  bake in the oven for 1 – 1½ hours until tender.

◎ To prepare the couscous place all of the ingredients into a bowl, add
  boiling stock and stir through. Leave for 5 minutes.

◎ Serve with the meat juices poured over the couscous.

- 🍃 **2, 3 and 4 Oven Aga,** cook in the Simmering Oven.
- 🍃 **Rayburn,** cook on the 4th set of runners in the Main Oven with the Thermodial reading Simmer.

Serve with...Nothing! You have everything you need here.

Variations

Moroccan lamb and mint couscous *Add 5 tbsp freshly chopped mint to the couscous before serving.*

James says...

This dish is full of protein with the lamb and chickpeas. It's fine to use cheaper cuts of lamb, but make sure you trim the fat off before cooking.

lasagne with a ton of basil.

An easy family favourite to make. Why not make double the quantity and freeze one? It takes the same amount of time to cook two as it does to cook one, so you'll save on fuel.

Ragú bolognaise
1 tbsp vegetable oil
1 onion, diced
2 cloves garlic, crushed
500g minced beef
200g mushrooms, sliced
2 tbsp tomato puree
1 x 400g can chopped tomatoes
Salt and freshly ground
black pepper
Large bunch fresh
basil, chopped.

White sauce
50g butter
50g plain flour
500ml milk
50g grated cheddar cheese
Salt and freshly ground
black pepper
To assemble
18 sheets fresh or dried
lasagne pasta
50g grated cheddar

Here's how to make it...

- Make the ragú bolognaise by using a heavy-based saucepan, heat the oil and sauté the onion until soft but not coloured. Add the garlic and mince and brown thoroughly.

- Add mushrooms and cook for 3–4 minutes. Add tomato puree and canned tomatoes, stir through and allow to simmer for 30 minutes. Season and add the basil.

- While the ragú is simmering make the white sauce. Melt butter in a pan and add the flour, cook for a few moments until it looks sandy in colour. Pour in a little milk at a time and stir through. Continue until all milk is absorbed and the sauce is smooth. Add the cheese and bring to the boil to thicken, stirring continually. Season.

- Preheat oven to 180°C (160°C if using a fan oven) or Gas Mark 4.
- To assemble, place 1/3 of the meat sauce in the bottom of a lasagne dish and top with sheets of lasagne. Cover with 1/3 of the white sauce and more sheets of lasagne. Repeat these layers until the dish is full. Top with grated cheddar. Bake for 30–45 minutes until firm in the middle and nice and golden on top.
- **2, 3 and 4 Oven Aga,** allow meat sauce to cook in the Simmering Oven for 30 minutes after adding the tomatoes. Make white sauce on the Simmering Plate and cook lasagne on the 4th set of runners in the Roasting Oven adding the Cold Plain Shelf if required.
- **Rayburn,** allow meat sauce to cook in the Lower Oven for 30 minutes after adding the tomatoes with the Thermodial reading Roast, or in the Main Oven with the Thermodial reading Simmer. Cook lasagne on the 4th set of runners in the Main Oven adding the Cold Plain Shelf if required with the Thermodial reading Roast.

Serve with... A fresh green salad.

Variations

Vegetable lasagne *Chop and sauté 1 carrot, 2 sticks celery, 3 peppers of mixed colours and 1 butternut squash to replace meat.*

Bacon and goats cheese lasagne *Add 150g bacon lardons to pan and fry with the onion. Replace cheddar with equal quantity goats cheese.*

James says...

Some makes of dried lasagne need to be boiled for 2-3 minutes to soften, so always read the instructions before making. Fresh pasta is good as it tastes better and is quicker to cook.

chilli con carne.

Growing up on a diet based mainly on potatoes means I'm not great with spicy food. Make this as hot and spicy as you like with more or less chilli.

1 tbsp vegetable oil
1 onion, diced
1 clove garlic, crushed
500g minced beef
1 tbsp vinegar
1 tbsp tomato puree
1 tbsp cumin

1 tbsp mild chilli powder
1 x 400g can chopped tomatoes
1 x 410g can kidney beans, drained
Salt and freshly ground black pepper

Here's how to make it...

🌀 Heat the oil in a large heavy-based saucepan and add the onion and garlic, sauté for 2–3 minutes until soft but not coloured. Add the mince and brown well.

🌀 In a small bowl, mix vinegar, tomato puree, cumin and chilli powder together and add to mince. Cook through for a few moments. Add tomatoes and kidney beans and reduce to a simmer for 30 minutes. Season and serve.

🌀 **2, 3 and 4 Oven Aga,** after adding the kidney beans, cook in the Simmering Oven for 30 minutes.

🌀 **Rayburn,** after adding the kidney beans, cook in the Lower Oven with the Thermodial reading Roast for 30 minutes or in the Main Oven with the Thermodial reading Simmer.

Serve with... Boiled white rice.

Variations

Mushroom chilli con carne *Add 200g sliced mushrooms to the chilli after browning the mince.*

Vegetable chilli *Replace mince with 500g diced vegetables including carrots, peppers, courgettes, squash, aubergine.*

James says...

Although I've used canned kidney beans, you can use dried ones. Steep them overnight, then boil rapidly for at least 20 minutes before simmering until tender. Red kidney beans contain a natural toxin that will make you very ill if they aren't given a good boil. The canning process removes this toxin.

moussaka.

My first impression of moussaka was not a good one. My mum is a Home Economics teacher back home in Northern Ireland. In the late 1980s, Mum was teaching an adult class entitled 'Hostess Cookery'. Moussaka was one of the dishes she brought home from the class for dinner and it was my first experience of aubergines. Yuck! Cook them properly and they are yummy; cook them poorly and it's like eating a slimy bath sponge.

Meat sauce	White sauce
1 tbsp vegetable oil	15g butter
1 onion, chopped	15g plain flour
1 clove garlic, crushed	300ml milk
500g minced lamb	Salt and freshly ground
150ml dry white wine	black pepper
150ml water	55g cheddar cheese, grated
1 x 400g can chopped tomatoes	Assembly
Pinch grated nutmeg	1 tbsp vegetable oil
Salt and freshly ground	1 medium aubergine, sliced
black pepper	1 large potato, peeled
	15g fresh breadcrumbs

Here's how to make it...

🌀 Make the meat sauce first. Using a heavy-based saucepan, heat the oil and sauté the onion until soft but not coloured. Add the garlic and mince and brown all over.

🌀 Add wine and water and cook for 3–4 minutes. Add canned tomatoes, nutmeg and seasoning, stir through and allow to simmer for 30 minutes.

🌀 Meanwhile, make the white sauce. Melt butter in a pan and add the flour. Cook for a few moments until it looks sandy in colour. Pour in a little milk at a time and stir through. Continue until all milk is absorbed and the sauce is smooth. Bring to the boil to thicken, stirring continually and then season.

- Heat the oil in a frying pan and fry the aubergine until coloured on each side. Boil the potato until tender and slice.
- Preheat oven to 180°C (160°C if using a fan oven) or Gas Mark 4.
- To assemble, cut the aubergine into thin disks and layer on the base of a casserole. Sprinkle with bread crumbs. Add half of the meat mixture and top with slices of potato. Add the rest of the meat mixture and top with more slices of potato. Top with sauce and sprinkle with grated cheddar. Bake for 1 hour 30 minutes until firm in the middle and nice and golden on top.
- **2, 3 and 4 Oven Aga,** allow meat sauce to cook in the Simmering Oven for 30 minutes. Make white sauce on the Simmering Plate and cook moussaka on the 4th set of runners in the Roasting Oven adding the Cold Plain Shelf if required.
- **Rayburn,** allow meat sauce to cook in the Lower Oven for 30 minutes with the Thermodial reading Roast or in the Main Oven with the Thermodial reading Simmer. Cook moussaka on the 4th set of runners in the Main Oven adding the Cold Plain Shelf if required with the Thermodial reading Roast.

Serve with... A fresh feta and dill salad.

Variations

Spicy moussaka *Add 1 tbsp medium chilli powder to meat sauce after adding the tomatoes.*

James says...

Salting aubergines is not usually necessary any more. We used to do it to remove the bitterness in aubergines when they weren't terribly fresh. If you find lots of seeds inside your cut aubergine, just sprinkle salt over the slices and leave to drain for 30 minutes before rinsing and cooking. If not many seeds are present, just cook it!

chicken and mushroom pie.

My mate Steve visits regularly for supper.
Steve likes this pie and has been badgering me
to include it in this book. It's good!

1 tbsp vegetable oil
1 onion, diced
1 clove garlic, crushed
500g chicken pieces or
diced chicken breast
200g mixed mushrooms, sliced

25g butter
25g plain flour
175ml milk
200g short crust (bought, or see
mix. page 34) or puff pastry

Here's how to make it...

- Using a heavy-based saucepan, heat the oil and sauté the onion until soft but not coloured. Add the garlic and chicken, brown well and add the mushrooms. Place the lid on, reduce the heat and cook for 20 minutes until tender.

- Preheat oven to 200°C (180°C if using a fan oven) or Gas Mark 6.

- Melt the butter in a pan, add the flour and cook for a few moments until sandy in colour. Add the milk a little at a time and stir well until smooth. Add the juices from the chicken and mushroom mixture, stir well.

- Place the chicken mixture into a dish and pour sauce on top. Roll out pastry and place on top. Make a hole in the top for steam to escape. Bake in the oven for 25–30 minutes until risen and golden.

- **2, 3 and 4 Oven Aga**, bake on the 4th set of runners in the Roasting Oven for 25–30 minutes until golden.

- **Rayburn**, bake on the 4th set of runners in the Main Oven for 25–30 minutes until golden with the Thermodial reading Roast.

Serve with... A rocket and baby spinach salad and some freshly cooked corn.

Variations

Chicken and wild mushroom pie *Add 50g dried wild mushrooms that have been steeping in 100ml boiling water for 20 minutes to mixture.*

James says...

In this recipe a velouté sauce has been used. Velouté is the name given to a sauce made with stock or cooking juices. It gives a lot more flavour to the finished dish.

steak and ale pie.

Great for cold winter nights.

1 tbsp vegetable oil
1 onion, chopped
1kg braising steak
3 tbsp plain flour
500ml ale

500ml beef stock made
with 2 stock cubes
2 carrots, peeled and sliced
2 tsp Dijon mustard
Ready rolled puff pastry

Here's how to make it...

- Heat the oil in a casserole dish and sauté the onion until soft but not coloured. Add the steak and cook until sealed.
- Add the flour and cook until absorbed and cooked through.
- Stir in the ale and then the stock, followed by the carrots and mustard.
- Bring to the boil and reduce to a simmer for 1 ½ hours.
- Preheat oven to 220°C (200°C if using a fan oven) or Gas Mark 6.
- Place puff pastry on top of meat casserole and cut a small hole to allow steam to escape. Bake for 25–30 minutes until pastry is risen and golden.
- **2, 3 and 4 Oven Aga,** cook on the 4th set of runners in the Roasting Oven for 25–30 minutes.
- **Rayburn,** cook on the 4th set of runners in the Main Oven with the Thermodial reading Roast for 25–30 minutes.

Serve with... Mashed potatoes and green vegetables.

Variations

Steak and Guinness pie Replace ale for an equivalent quantity of Guinness.

James says...

It's a lot of hassle to make puff pastry. Why not buy it when it's reduced in the supermarket and freeze until needed? Any puff pastry that's left can be re-rolled and used again.

chicken fajitas.

There is a small but very noisy Mexican restaurant in Clapham where I live. The fajitas are the best I have ever had.

3 tbsp vegetable oil	2 tsp dried oregano
2 onions, roughly sliced	1 tsp cinnamon powder
3 peppers of mixed	1 tsp mild chilli powder
colours, roughly sliced	1 tsp cayenne pepper or paprika
2 chicken breasts, sliced	Zest and freshly squeezed
into thin strips	juice of 2 limes

Here's how to make it...

- Heat a frying or sauté pan with the oil until it's nice and hot. Sauté the onion and pepper for 5–6 minutes until the onion starts to colour.
- Add the chicken and cook until tender.
- Add oregano, cinnamon, chilli, cayenne and zest and juice of limes. Cook until aromatic.
- **2, 3 and 4 Oven Aga,** cook on the Boiling Plate.
- **Rayburn,** cook on the hot end of the hotplate with a rising heat.

Serve with...
Grated cheddar, guacamole, re-fried beans, soured cream and tomato salsa all wrapped up in a warm tortilla.

Variations
Steak fajitas *Replace chicken with steak.*
Prawn fajitas *Replace chicken with large peeled prawns.*

James says...
To warm the tortillas, either place onto a plate in the microwave for 30 seconds or wrapped in kitchen foil in the oven for 10 minutes.

tagliatelle and meat balls.

A bit of European fusion food — Swedish meatballs with Italian pasta.

Meatballs
500g lean minced beef
60g white breadcrumbs
1 garlic clove, crushed
2 tbsp fresh parsley, chopped
1 tsp dried oregano
Large pinch freshly grated nutmeg
¼ tsp ground coriander

Salt and freshly ground black pepper
4 tbsp vegetable oil
Sauce
3 tbsp olive oil
1 large onion, sliced
2 sticks celery, sliced
2 cloves garlic, crushed
1 x 400g can chopped tomatoes
2 tbsp tomato puree
400g cooked tagliatelle

Here's how to make it...

- To make the meatballs, combine all the ingredients and mix well. Using floured hands divide the mixture into 12 and roll into balls. Heat the oil in a pan and fry for 10 minutes turning regularly.
- To make the sauce, heat the oil in a pan and sauté the onion, celery and garlic until soft but not coloured.
- Add all the remaining ingredients and cook through. Allow to simmer for 5 minutes.
- To assemble, divide the tagliatelle between serving plates, top with meatballs and sauce.

Serve with... Freshly grated Parmesan.

Variations

Tagliatelle with pork and coriander meat balls *Use pork instead of beef mince and add 2 tsp ground coriander.*

James says...

Why not try different coloured pasta?

devilled chicken supremes.

Devilled means spicy, not evil!

4 chicken supremes	1 garlic clove, crushed
1 tbsp apricot jam	1 tbsp Worcestershire sauce
1 tsp Dijon mustard	3 tbsp tomato ketchup
1 tsp cayenne pepper	1 tbsp soy sauce

Here's how to make it...

- Preheat oven to 200°C (180°C if using a fan oven) or Gas Mark 6. Grease a baking sheet.
- Place all of the ingredients into a bowl and mix together until well coated.
- Turn out onto a baking tray and roast for 45 minutes.
- **2, 3 and 4 Oven Aga,** cook on the 3rd set of runners in the Roasting Oven for 45 minutes.
- **Rayburn,** cook on the 4th set of runners in the Main Oven with the Thermodial reading Roast for 45 minutes.

Variations

Devilled sausages *Replace the chicken with pork sausages.*
....
Devilled pork chops *Replace the chicken with pork chops.*
....

James says...

If the meat starts to brown a bit too much, cover with kitchen foil.

prawn, orange and ginger stir-fry.

Such a quick stir fry that's bright in colour and full of flavour.

1 tbsp toasted sesame oil
1 tbsp sunflower oil
5cm fresh root ginger, peeled and finely sliced
2 cloves garlic, finely chopped
1 tsp dried chillies

Salt and freshly ground black pepper
500g peeled raw tiger prawns
1 large red pepper, sliced
2 large spring onions, sliced diagonally
2 large oranges, segmented

Here's how to make it...

💧 Heat a wok until it's nice and hot and add the oils.

💧 Add all ingredients except the prawns and orange and stir fry for 2–3 minutes.

💧 Add prawns and orange, stir fry for 1 minute. Serve.

💧 **2, 3 and 4 Oven Aga,** Stir-fry on the Boiling Plate.

💧 **Rayburn,** Stir-fry on the hot end of the hotplate with the Thermodial reading Roast.

Serve with... Freshly cooked cellophane noodles.

Variations

Chicken, orange and ginger stir-fry *Replace the prawns with chicken strips but cook in the hot oil before adding ginger and vegetables.*

Pork, orange and ginger stir-fry *Replace the prawns with pork strips but cook in the hot oil before adding ginger and vegetables.*

James says...

To segment an orange, cut the top and bottom off, cut the sides away past the pith (the white bit) and using a small knife cut into each segment so it falls out.

coq au vin.

It literally means 'rooster in wine'.

15g butter
8 shallots, peeled
5 cloves garlic, crushed
8 chicken thighs on the
bone, skin removed
2 tsp dried thyme

150g streaky bacon,
roughly chopped
200g button mushrooms
500ml red wine
500ml chicken stock
Salt and freshly ground
black pepper

Here's how to make it...

🌾 Preheat oven to 220°C (200°C if using a fan oven) or Gas Mark 7.

🌾 Heat a cast iron casserole dish on the hob and melt the butter. Add
the shallots and garlic and cook for a few moments until browned.
Add the chicken and cook for 5 minutes.

🌾 Add the thyme and bacon and cook for another 5 minutes.

🌾 Add all other ingredients and bring to the boil. Place into the oven for
1 hour.

🌾 **2, 3 and 4 Oven Aga,** cook in the Simmering Oven for 1 hour.

🌾 **Rayburn,** cook in the Lower Oven with the Thermodial reading Roast
or in the Main Oven with the Thermodial reading Simmer for 1 hour.

Serve with...Olive oil mashed potatoes.

Variations

Venison and pork in wine Buy venison in season and it isn't too
expensive. Use 250g stewing venison and 250g diced leg or shoulder of
pork instead of the chicken.

James says...

I'm sure most people think of stock as a cube or
something difficult a chef makes in a kitchen. In the
supermarket, pouches of liquid stock are available.
A liquid will hold more flavour than a dried cube.

simple fish pie.

There is something about potatoes and my diet. Growing up in Northern Ireland (or Norn Iron as we call it) means potatoes need to feature in every meal. Forgive me.

500g cooked fish　　　　　　　　　*25g grated cheddar cheese*
500g mashed potato

Here's how to make it...

- 🌙 Preheat oven to 220°C (200°C if using a fan oven) or Gas Mark 8.
- 🌙 Flake the fish and remove any bones. Mix with potato.
- 🌙 Place into a dish and smooth over. Top with grated cheese and place into the oven for 25 minutes until brown and crispy.
- 🌙 **2, 3 and 4 Oven Aga,** cook on the 4th set of runners in the Roasting Oven for 25 minutes adding the Cold Plain Shelf if necessary.
- 🌙 **Rayburn,** cook on the 4th set of runners in the Main Oven with the Thermodial reading Roast for 25 minutes adding the Cold Plain Shelf if necessary.

Serve with... Parsley sauce and vegetables.

Variations

Russian fish pie *Make a white sauce by melting 25g butter and adding 25g plain flour. Cook until sandy in colour and gently stir in 250ml milk a bit at a time to make a smooth sauce. Bring to the boil to thicken. Add fish and place in a dish. Cover with puff pastry and bake for 25 minutes.*

James says...

Canned fish can be used instead of fresh. Also, to save money, why not use the cheapest cuts of fish or defrosted frozen fish?

chicken á la king.

A classic British recipe, I made it for my GCSE course work in 1994.

1.5kg cooked chicken
50g butter
100g mushrooms, sliced
1 green pepper, diced
1 carrot, peeled and
cut into batons
1 tbsp plain flour
500ml chicken stock
150ml milk

Here's how to make it...

- Remove the skin and bones from the chicken and cut into bite sized pieces.
- Melt the butter and fry the mushrooms, pepper and carrot until the mushrooms are soft. Add the flour and cook through.
- Gradually add the stock and milk until smooth and add the chicken. Bring to the boil and reduce to a simmer for 5–6 minutes.

Serve with... Freshly boiled white or brown rice.

Variations

Smokey chicken á la king *Add 1 tbsp smoked paprika when adding the flour.*

James says...

This is a super quick, 15-minute supper dish.

pancetta, pork and pea risotto.

It only takes one pan and is cooked in 20 minutes.

1 tbsp vegetable oil
1 onion, chopped
1 clove garlic, crushed
150g pancetta or bacon lardons
1 tsp dried sage
350g minced pork

275g risotto rice
125ml white wine
75g frozen peas, defrosted
700ml beef stock made
with 3 stock cubes
Salt and freshly ground
black pepper

Here's how to make it...

- Heat oil in a heavy-based pan and add the onion and garlic. Sauté for 2–3 minutes until soft but not coloured. Add the pancetta or lardons and cook until crispy.
- Stir in sage.
- Add the minced pork and cook until sealed. Add the rice and stir through for a few moments.
- Add the wine and peas and mix through. Pour in the stock – about a quarter of it at a go – stirring well between each addition. Leave to simmer for 20 minutes until all of the liquid has been absorbed, season.
- **2, 3 and 4 Oven Aga,** after adding stock, cover and place into the Simmering Oven for 20 minutes.
- **Rayburn,** after adding stock, cover and place into the Lower Oven with the Thermodial reading Roast for 20 minutes, or in the Main Oven with the Thermodial reading Simmer.

Serve with... Freshly grated Parmesan or Pecorino cheese.

Variations

Porcini, pork and pea risotto *Allow 50g dried porcini mushrooms to steep in boiling water for 20 minutes before adding to risotto to replace prosciutto or lardons.*

James says...

Full of strong flavours, this risotto is also great for a dinner party.

venison casserole.

Vacuum packed off-cuts of venison are easily available in large supermarkets and this makes a great family meal.

1 tbsp vegetable oil	6 juniper berries, crushed
1 red onion, diced	½ glass port
250g venison cut into bite-sized pieces	½ bottle red wine
250g pork cut into bite-sized pieces	150ml beef stock
25g seasoned flour	2 carrots peeled and sliced
	1 parsnip peeled and sliced
	2 tbsp red currant jelly

Here's how to make it...

🌢 Preheat oven to 150°C (130°C if using a fan oven) or Gas Mark 2.

🌢 Heat a cast iron casserole dish on the hob with the oil and sauté the onion until soft but not coloured.

🌢 Toss the venison and pork in the seasoned flour. Add to casserole and brown in batches.

🌢 Add juniper, port, red wine and stock. Bring to the boil.

🌢 Add carrots and parsnips.

🌢 Place into the oven for 2 hours, stirring occasionally.

🌢 Stir through red currant jelly and serve.

🌢 **2, 3 and 4 Oven Aga,** cover and cook in the Simmering Oven for 2 hours.

🌢 **Rayburn,** cover and cook on the 4th set of runners in the Main Oven with the Thermodial reading Simmer or in the Lower Oven with the Thermodial reading Roast for 2 hours.

Serve with... Dauphinoise potatoes or a good hearty wholegrain mustard mash.

Variations

Venison and walnut casserole *Add 50g pickled walnuts to casserole.*

James says...

Venison is a strong tasting meat so it's best to use equal parts pork to venison otherwise it can be too gamey in flavour.

stuffed bacon rolls.

Mum used to make these for our family when I was small. They are very easy to make, cost effective and filling.

1 tbsp vegetable oil
½ onion, finely chopped
500g fresh breadcrumbs
1 coarsely grated apple

2 tbsp freshly chopped parsley
or 1 tbsp dried parsley
2 eggs, beaten
8 slices bacon

Here's how to make it...

- Preheat oven to 190°C (170°C if using a fan oven) or Gas Mark 5.
- Heat the oil in a large pan and add the onion, sauté until soft but not coloured.
- Add breadcrumbs, apple and parsley, mix well, turn off the heat. Allow to cool for a few moments.
- Mix the egg in and divide stuffing into 8. Make a ball of stuffing and place on the large end of a slice of bacon. Roll up and secure with a cocktail stick. Place onto a baking dish and cook for 30–35 minutes until the outside of the bacon is crispy.
- **2, 3 and 4 Oven Aga,** cook on the 4th set of runners in the Roasting Oven for 30–35 minutes.
- **Rayburn,** cook on the 4th set of runners in the Main Oven with the Thermodial reading Roast for 30–35 minutes.

Serve with... Oven chips and sweetcorn.

Variations

Apple and stilton bacon rolls Add 30g crumbled stilton after adding the egg.
Apricot and walnut bacon rolls Add 30g chopped ready to eat dried apricots and 15g walnut pieces.

James says...

If the bacon rolls are starting to brown too much, cover the top of the dish with some kitchen foil.

chicken casserole.

Comfort food at its very best.

1 tbsp vegetable oil
1 onion finely diced
8 chicken thighs, trimmed

3 carrots peeled and sliced
100g mushrooms, sliced
1 x 200g can sweet corn
200ml chicken stock

Here's how to make it...

- Preheat oven to 200°C (180°C if using a fan oven) or Gas Mark 6.
- Using a cast iron casserole, heat the oil and soften the onion for a few minutes without colouring it.
- Seal the chicken for a few moments and add the carrots, mushrooms and sweet corn. Add stock and bring to the boil. Cover and place into the oven for 1 hour.
- Remove the lid and allow the chicken skin to crisp in the oven for 15 minutes.
- **2, 3 and 4 Oven Aga,** cook in the Simmering Oven for 1 hour and then move to the 4th set of runners in the Roasting Oven for 15 minutes.
- **Rayburn,** cook in the Lower Oven with the Thermodial reading Roast for 1 hour and then move to the 4th set of runners in the Main Oven for 15 minutes.

Serve with... Potato champ. That's a Northern Irish dish of mashed potatoes with spring onions, or scallions as we call them.

Variations

Chicken and apricot casserole *Add 50g of whole ready to eat apricots to dish before adding stock.*

James says...

If you don't like chicken skin, remove it. I keep it on as it adds texture and flavour to the dish. If you do decide to remove it, put it in the casserole so the flavour permeates the dish while cooking and discard before serving.

spaghetti carbonara.

Smoked bacon in a creamy sauce... serious comfort food.

175g smoked bacon
lardons or pancetta
2 tbsp vegetable oil
3 garlic cloves, crushed

3 eggs, beaten
50g grated Parmesan
Salt and freshly ground
black pepper
400g spaghetti, cooked

Here's how to make it...

- Heat a large deep frying pan over a medium heat and add the oil and lardons or pancetta. Cook for a few minutes until crispy. Add the garlic and cook for a moment or so.
- Take the pan off the heat and add the freshly cooked spaghetti, mix through and add the egg and Parmesan, mix through to combine, the heat from the pan should be enough to cook the egg.

Serve with... Freshly chopped parsley to garnish.

Variations

Spaghetti prawn carbonara *Replace the bacon with 100g thawed frozen prawns, but don't fry them, just toss them in the oil to heat through before adding the garlic.*

James says...

If the egg is not cooking through, turn the mixture gently on a low heat.

beef curry.

Make as hot as you like by adjusting the amount or type of curry powder. If you like it very hot, try a vindaloo.

1 tbsp vegetable oil
500g stewing steak, fat trimmed off and cut into bite-sized pieces
1 onion, diced
2 tbsp mild curry powder
25g plain flour

15g tomato puree
500ml vegetable stock
2 tbsp mango chutney
1 tbsp desiccated coconut
1 tbsp sultanas
1 small apple, peeled, cored and chopped

Here's how to make it...

- Preheat oven to 200°C (180°C if using a fan oven) or Gas Mark 6.
- Heat the oil in a heavy-based pan and fry the meat until brown. Add the onion and sweat for 10 minutes. Drain off any excess fat.
- Add the curry powder and flour, cook for 2 minutes.
- Add tomato puree and stock, stir well, add remaining ingredients and bring to the boil.
- Cook in the oven for 1½–2 hours until tender.
- **2, 3 and 4 Oven Aga,** cook in the Simmering Oven for 1½–2 hours.
- **Rayburn,** cook the Lower Oven with the Thermodial reading Roast or in the Main Oven with the Thermodial reading Simmer.

Serve with... Boiled basmati rice.

Variations

Chicken curry *Replace beef with chicken.*
....
Pork curry *Replace beef with pork.*
....

James says...

Make a double quantity and freeze.

braised lamb shanks in red wine and balsamic.

A few years ago I was invited to a friend's in Oxfordshire for the weekend. It was a cold winter's day. I arrived to find lamb shanks in the oven for dinner. What a great way to spend the evening with a good bottle of red!

1 tbsp vegetable oil
1 onion, diced
2 cloves garlic, crushed
4 lamb shanks
12 shallots, peeled

1 bottle red wine
150ml vegetable stock, made with 2 stock cubes
2 carrots peeled and sliced
1 tbsp balsamic vinegar

Here's how to make it...

- Preheat oven to 150°C (130°C if using a fan oven) or Gas Mark 2.
- Heat the oil in a cast iron casserole dish and sauté the onion and garlic until soft but without colour. Add the lamb shanks and seal all over.
- Add the shallots, wine, stock, carrots and vinegar. Bring to the boil and place in the oven for 2 hours until tender.
- 2, 3 and 4 Oven Aga, cook in the Simmering Oven for 2 hours.
- Rayburn, cook in the Lower Oven with the Thermodial reading Roast or in the Main Oven with the Thermodial reading Simmer for 2 hours.

Serve with... Mashed potatoes and roasted red peppers.

Variations

Braised lamb shanks with parsnips *Replace carrots with parsnips.*

James says...

Shallots are fiddly things to peel. The easiest way I have found to do it is to pop them in boiling water for a few minutes. The skins just rub off!

sweet and sour pork.

One of Britain's favourite takeaways. Why not do it at home? It's really easy!

Sweet and sour sauce
2 tbsp light soy sauce
2 tbsp caster sugar
2 tbsp tomato ketchup
100ml pineapple juice
2 tbsp distilled vinegar
1 tbsp cornflour dissolved in 4 tbsp water
1 carrot, peeled and very thinly sliced
1 red pepper, roughly chopped

Batter
100g plain flour
3 tbsp baking powder
1 egg white, lightly beaten
1 tbsp vegetable oil
100ml warm water
200ml vegetable oil
300g diced pork, cut into bite sized pieces

Here's how to make it...

- Prepare the sauce by combining all ingredients in a small bowl. Set aside.
- Combine all of the ingredients for the batter in a bowl and whisk together until smooth. The batter should not be runny, but should drop off a spoon.
- Heat the oil in a deep frying pan and dip the pork into the batter. When the oil is hot, cook the pork in small batches for 5–6 minutes and drain on kitchen paper.
- Heat the sauce in a saucepan until hot.
- **2, 3 and 4 Oven Aga,** heat the oil on the Simmering Plate until hot and then move to the Boiling Plate. As the Boiling Plate is over 300°C the oil may spit.

🍳 **Rayburn,** heat the oil on the cooler end of the hotplate with the Thermodial rising from Bake to Roast and move to the hot end for frying. The Rayburn hotplate is always hottest on a rising heat.

Serve with...fried rice.

Variations

Sweet and sour chicken *Replace pork with chicken.*

James says...

By adding the baking powder, the batter will puff up and become fluffy.

kedgeree.

Kedgeree was brought back by British colonials from India and was introduced to the UK in Victorian times as a breakfast dish.

250g basmati rice
50g butter
500g cooked smoked haddock or salmon
Salt and freshly ground black pepper

1 tbsp Madras curry powder
2 hard boiled eggs
Lemon wedges and freshly chopped parsley to serve

Here's how to make it...

- Bring rice to the boil in a pan with salted water, boil for 10–12 minutes until just cooked. Drain.
- Melt the butter in a pan and toss rice and fish in it. Season and add curry powder.
- Chop 1 egg and add to rice and fish mix, stir through. Cut second egg into quarters and set aside.
- Place kedgeree into a serving dish and garnish with parsley, egg quarters and lemon wedges.
- **2, 3 and 4 Oven Aga,** bring the rice to the boil, place lid on top of pan and place into the Simmering Oven for 10 minutes.
- **Rayburn,** bring the rice to the boil, place lid on top of pan and place into the Lower Oven for 10 minutes with the Thermodial reading Roast, or into the Main Oven with the Thermodial reading Simmer. Alternatively, boil on top with a rising heat.

Serve with... Freshly squeezed orange juice. It's a breakfast dish after all.

Variations

Smoked trout kedgeree *Replace the haddock with smoked trout and stir through 1 tbsp sliced almonds after cooking.*

Pesto kedgeree *Stir through 1 tbsp fresh pesto before serving.*

James says...

Kedgeree can be served hot or cold.

penne arrabiata.

Hot and spicy pasta sauce. Kind of a boy thing!

1 tbsp vegetable oil
1 onion, finely chopped
4 cloves garlic, crushed

3 red chillies, chopped
1 green pepper, diced
2 x 400g tins chopped tomatoes
1 tbsp balsamic vinegar

Here's how to make it...

- Heat the oil in a heavy-based saucepan and add the onion and garlic, sauté for 5 minutes until soft but not coloured.
- Add garlic, chillies and pepper, cook for 2–3 minutes.
- Add remaining ingredients, stir well and simmer for 5–6 minutes.

Serve with... Freshly cooked penne pasta.

Variations

Spicy salami arrabiata Add 100g chopped spicy salami.

James says...

This sauce freezes well and is very quick to make.

sole florentine.

The word florentine in a recipe usually means
the dish contains spinach.

250g frozen or fresh spinach
4 tbsp cream
Salt and freshly ground
black pepper
Large pinch grated nutmeg

4 dover or lemon sole fillets
Freshly squeezed juice
of half a lemon
1 tbsp Parmesan

Here's how to make it...

- Preheat oven to 180°C (160°C if using a fan oven) or Gas Mark 4.
- Cook the spinach in boiling water for 5–6 minutes, drain well and squeeze dry. Place into a mixing bowl with cream, seasoning and nutmeg, mix thoroughly.
- Spoon half of the spinach mixture onto the bottom of a baking dish and place the fish on top, sprinkle with lemon juice. Place the remaining spinach on top, sprinkle with Parmesan and cover with foil.
- Bake for 10–15 minutes until fish is cooked.
- **2, 3 and 4 Oven Aga,** cook on the 4th set of runners in the Roasting Oven for 7–10 minutes.
- **Rayburn,** cook on the 4th set of runners in the Main Oven with the Thermodial reading Bake.

Serve with... Potatoes and corn on the cob.

Variations

Skate florentine *Use skate wings instead of sole.*

James says...

Fish is really quick to cook, the moisture from the spinach will help steam the fish when it's in the oven.

jambalaya.

For this dish you can add in lots of left overs to use up what's in the fridge.

2 tbsp vegetable oil
1 onion, chopped
3 mixed coloured peppers, diced
2 cloves garlic, crushed
100g chorizo, diced
400g chicken breast, cut
into bite sized pieces

2 Scotch Bonnet chillies,
finely chopped
500g easy-to-cook white rice
1 tsp chilli powder
2 tbsp Cajun or Jerk spice
1 litre chicken stock
450g prawns

Here's how to make it...

- Using a large deep sided pan heat the oil and add the onion, peppers, garlic and chorizo and cook until the onion is soft. Add the chicken and cook until the outsides turn white.

- Add all other ingredients except stock and prawns and cook to release flavour for 1 minute. Add stock, bring to the boil.

- Reduce to a simmer and cook for 15 minutes. Add prawns and cook for a further 5 minutes.

- 2, 3 and 4 Oven Aga, bring to the boil, place the lid on top and place into the Simmering Oven for 15 minutes, add the prawns and return it to the oven for another 5 minutes.

- Rayburn, bring to the boil, place the lid on top and cook on the 4th set of runners in the Main Oven with the Thermodial reading Simmer for 15 minutes, add the prawns and return it to the oven for another 5 minutes.

Serve with... Just on its own.

Variations

Vegetarian jambalaya *Replace the chorizo, chicken and prawns with chickpeas, sweetcorn and diced butternut squash.*

James says...

Scotch Bonnet chillies are extremely hot. Replace with milder ones if you prefer.

bœuf bourguignon.

A classic French dish that never fails to impress!

50g butter	150ml beef stock
6 rashers streaky bacon, chopped	1 bottle full bodied red wine
1 kg lean braising steak, trimmed	1 bouquet garni
1 clove garlic, crushed	6 shallots, peeled
3 tbsp seasoned plain flour	150g button mushrooms

Here's how to make it...

- Preheat oven to 170°C (150°C if using a fan oven) or Gas Mark 3.
- Heat the butter in a casserole dish and fry the bacon until crispy. Remove from casserole and set aside.
- Add the meat to the pan and seal on all sides. Add garlic and fry for a few moments. Stir in flour and cook for 2–3 minutes.
- Add stock and wine and stir through. Bring to the boil.
- Add bouquet garni, shallots and mushrooms. Place lid on casserole and cook in the oven for 2 hours until tender.
- **2, 3 and 4 Oven Aga,** cook in the Simmering Oven for 2 hours.
- **Rayburn,** cook in the Lower Oven with the Thermodial reading Roast or in the Main Oven with the Thermodial reading Simmer for 2 hours.

Serve with... Potatoes and vegetables.

Variations
Beef Somerset *Replace wine with a nice fruity cider. Great cost savings and just as delicious!.*

James says...

When using an Aga or Rayburn, always make sure you've got the casserole boiling well before moving to the oven.

teriyaki beef stir-fry.

In 2004 I spent four weeks in Japan at the World Home Economics Congress. Japan is very different to the UK. The toilets wash and dry you (that was a shock!) but the food is fantastic.

Marinade
4 tbsp light soy sauce
4 tbsp medium sherry
1 clove garlic, finely chopped
2 tbsp freshly grated ginger

450g beef fillet, sliced
2 tbsp groundnut oil
1 large carrot, cut into match sticks (julienne)
1 cucumber, deseeded and cut into match sticks (julienne)
4 spring onions, trimmed and sliced diagonally

Here's how to make it...

- Prepare the marinade by placing all of the ingredients into a bowl. Add the meat and cover, place into the fridge for at least one hour.
- Heat a wok until very hot, add the oil and once hot add the beef and marinade. Stir-fry for 5–6 minutes until cooked.
- Add the vegetables and stir-fry for a few moments. Serve.
- 2, 3 and 4 Oven Aga, stir fry on the Boiling Plate.
- Rayburn, stir fry on the hot end of the hotplate on a rising heat.

Serve with... Boiled egg noodles that have been quickly fried in toasted sesame oil.

Variations

Teriyaki salmon stir-fry *Replace beef with thinly sliced salmon fillets.*

Teriyaki chicken stir-fry *Replace beef with thin chicken breast strips.*

Teriyaki pork stir-fry *Replace beef with thin pork strips.*

James says...

For most hobs a wok with a flat base is better than a round one as there is a greater surface area to heat. Hard anodised woks heat up very quickly whereas a stainless steel one will take longer.

carbonade de bœuf.

This is a classic French dish of beef braised in beer and red onions.

2 tbsp vegetable oil	300ml beef stock
2 onions, thinly sliced	1 bay leaf
1kg braising steak, trimmed	1 tbsp dried thyme
4 cloves garlic, crushed	Salt and freshly ground
2 tbsp light brown sugar	black pepper
3 tbsp plain flour	2 tbsp cider or white
500ml lager	wine vinegar

Here's how to make it...

- Preheat oven to 150°C (130°C if using a fan oven) or Gas Mark 2.
- Heat the oil in a casserole dish and sauté the onion until soft but not coloured. Add the meat and garlic and cook until the meat is browned.
- Add sugar and flour and cook through.
- Gradually add lager and stock and stir until smooth.
- Add bay leaf, thyme seasoning and vinegar. Bring to the boil and place in the oven for 2 hours until tender.
- **2, 3 and 4 Oven Aga,** cook in the Simmering Oven for 2 hours.
- **Rayburn,** cook in the Lower Oven with the Thermodial reading Roast or in the Main Oven with the Thermodial reading Simmer for 2 hours.

Serve with... Potatoes and freshly cooked seasonal vegetables.

Variations

Rich carbonade de bœuf *Replace the lager with stout for an even fuller, richer flavour.*

James says...

During cooking all the alcohol will be driven off to leave the flavour of the beer.

coley and lemongrass with a parsley sauce.

Coley is a white fish with the texture and flavour of cod, but cheaper and more sustainable. It's slightly grey in colour before cooking but is white when cooked.

4 coley fillets, skinned
2 sticks lemongrass, bruised

Parsley sauce
15g butter
15g plain flour
250ml milk
5 tbsp fresh parsley, chopped
Salt and pepper

Here's how to make it...

- Wrap all 4 coley fillets in a large piece of kitchen foil to make a large parcel with the bruised lemongrass on top of the fish.
- Place into a steamer for 10 minutes until opaque.
- Meanwhile prepare the sauce by melting the butter in a saucepan, stir in the flour and cook for a few moments until sandy in colour. Add the milk a little at a time until smooth. Add the parsley and bring to the boil, stirring until thickened. Season to taste.

Serve with... Boiled potatoes and carrots. Why not boil the carrots with the juice of a lemon added to the cooking water?.

Variations

Cod and lemongrass with a parsley sauce Replace the coley with cod fillets.

James says...

By adding lemon juice to the cooking water the carrots take on a slightly different flavour, but be warned, they will take an extra 5 minutes to cook.

rich braised beef with herb dumplings.

A great stew that's best served the following day to allow deep flavours to develop.

2 x 440ml can stout
25g dried porcini mushrooms
1 tbsp vegetable oil
2 onions, thickly sliced
2 large carrots, thickly sliced
1kg shin or skirt of beef
125g bacon lardons
1 tbsp dried thyme
1 tbsp dried parsley
1 bay leaf
6 allspice berries, crushed

2 cloves garlic, crushed
Salt and freshly ground black pepper
Luting paste
225g plain white flour
150ml water
Dumpling mix
175g self raising flour
Pinch of salt
75g suet
2 tbsp fresh parsley, chopped

Here's how to make it...

- Preheat oven to 150°C (130°C if using a fan oven) or Gas Mark 2.
- Pour stout and dried mushrooms into a shallow pan, bring to the boil and reduce by half.
- Place a casserole dish onto the hob and heat the oil until hot, add the carrots and onions, reduce the heat and sweat with the lid on for 10 minutes.
- Add beef and lardons, cook to seal the meat.
- Add herbs, spices, garlic, seasoning, stout and mushrooms. Bring to the boil.
- To make the luting paste, mix flour with water to make a smooth dough. Wet the edges of the casserole dish and place the lid on top. Roll the dough into a long sausage shape and place all the way around the seal of the casserole. Place into the oven for 3 hours.

- ⊘ To make the dumplings, mix all of the ingredients together with enough chilled water to bind into a dough. Divide mixture into 12 and roll into balls with floured hands. Bring a pan of stock to the boil and simmer dumplings for 30 minutes.

- ⊘ **2, 3 and 4 Oven Aga,** cook in the Simmering Oven for 3 hours. Bring dumplings to the boil and place into the Simmering Oven for 30 minutes.

- ⊘ **Rayburn,** cook in the Lower Oven with the Thermodial reading Roast or in the Main Oven with the Thermodial reading Simmer for 3 hours. To cook the dumplings, bring a pan of stock to the boil and place into the Lower Oven for 30 minutes.

Serve with... Fresh green vegetables.

Variations

Rich braised venison with herb dumplings *Replace the beef with diced stewing venison.*

Rich braised beef with herb and mustard dumplings *Add 1 tbsp English mustard powder to dumpling mix.*

James says...
Luting paste seals all of the moisture into the food and keeps the casserole very moist.

thai chicken curry.

It's sad I know. I was flying to Sydney for
New Year and had a 90-minute stop-over in
Bangkok airport. So I had a Thai curry. It was
very similar to the ones we get in the UK.

Spice mix

4 cloves
1 tsp coriander seeds
1 tsp cumin seeds
Seeds from 3 cardamom pods

Rempah

2 garlic cloves, crushed
2 tbsp finely grated fresh ginger
2 stalks lemongrass, bruised
1 onion, roughly chopped

1 tbsp sunflower oil
1 tbsp sesame oil
1 tbsp curry paste
1 tsp turmeric
400g chicken breast cut
into bite-sized pieces
4 tomatoes, quartered
300ml coconut milk
150ml vegetable stock
4 red chillies, bruised

Here's how to make it...

- Place the cloves, coriander, cumin and cardamom seeds into a small heavy-based pan and dry fry for 2–3 minutes until aromatic. Cool and grind to a powder.

- To make the rempah, place the garlic, ginger, lemongrass and onion into a blender and puree until smooth. Heat both oils in a large pan.

- Fry onion paste with curry powder and powdered spices for a few moments. Add the chicken and cook for about 5 minutes until sealed. Add all remaining ingredients and simmer for 20–25 minutes until cooked.

Serve with...Thai jasmine rice.

Variations

Nutty Thai curry *Add a handful of cashew nuts before serving.*

Thai beef curry *Replace chicken with beef.*

Thai fish curry *Add chunks of white fish or salmon during the last 5 minutes of cooking.*

James says...

Although large chillies can be used, small bird's eye chillies give a greater kick.

beef goulash.

A Hungarian dish.

1 kg stewing steak cut
into bite-sized pieces
2 tbsp plain flour, seasoned
3 tbsp vegetable oil
1 onion, finely chopped
225g pancetta or bacon lardons

2 cloves garlic, crushed
4 tbsp paprika
1 x 400g can peeled
plum tomatoes
300ml beef stock
150ml soured cream

Here's how to make it...

- Preheat oven to 170°C (150°C if using a fan oven) or Gas Mark 3.
- Toss the beef in the seasoned flour. Heat the oil in a large casserole dish. Fry onions until soft and slightly golden.
- Add pancetta or lardons, garlic and paprika and fry until crispy. Add the meat in batches until browned on all sides.
- Add the tomatoes and stock and bring to the boil. Place into the oven for 1 hour.
- Remove from the oven and stir through soured cream.
- 2, 3 and 4 Oven Aga, cook in the Simmering Oven for 1 hour.
- Rayburn, cook in the Lower Oven with the Thermodial reading Roast or in the Main Oven with the Thermodial reading Simmer for 1 hour.

Serve with...Buttered noodles.

Variations

Chicken goulash *Use 500g of diced chicken thigh meat instead of beef.*

James says...

To give a smokier flavour, replace the paprika with smoked paprika.

steak and kidney pie.

A British classic.

700g stewing steak, trimmed
and cut into bite-sized pieces
225g ox kidneys, white core
removed and cut into 1cm chunks
4 tbsp plain white
flour, seasoned

3 tbsp vegetable oil
1 onion, finely chopped
450ml beef stock
200g mushrooms, sliced
Ready rolled puff pastry

Here's how to make it...

- Preheat oven to 170°C (150°C if using a fan oven) or Gas Mark 3.
- Toss meat and kidneys in seasoned flour.
- Heat oil in a casserole and sauté the onion until soft but not coloured. Add the meat and kidneys in batches and cook until sealed.
- Add all other ingredients and bring to the boil. Place lid on casserole and bake for 1 ½ hours until tender.
- Increase the oven temperature to 200°C (180°C if using a fan oven) or Gas Mark 6.
- Remove from oven and place into a large open topped dish and cover with pastry. Make a hole in the centre to allow steam to escape.
- 2, 3 and 4 Oven Aga, cook in the Simmering Oven for 1½ hours and then move to the 4th set of runners in the Roasting Oven to cook the pastry.
- Rayburn, cook on the 4th set of runners in the Main Oven with the Thermodial reading Simmer, then increase the heat to Roast to cook the pastry.

Serve with... Fresh green vegetables.

Variations

Rich steak and kidney pie *Add 100ml port to meat when adding stock.*

James says...

It's important to remove the white core (nephrons) from the kidneys as it tastes bitter.

paella.

A delicious Mediterranean classic!

2 tbsp olive oil
100g chorizo, peeled and
chopped into small cubes
2 chicken breasts, cut
into 2.5cm pieces
1 onion, finely sliced
1 red pepper, diced
2 garlic cloves, crushed
350g paella rice
150ml white wine

1 x 2g packet saffron, mixed
with 3 tbsp hot water
1l chicken stock
100g raw tiger prawns,
shells removed
100g raw squid rings
12 large mussels, washed
6 large king prawns, in shells
Juice 1 lemon
4tbsp chopped fresh parsley

Here's how to make it...

- Heat 1 tbsp of oil in large pan. Add the chorizo and brown for about 3-4 minutes. Add the chicken and continue to brown all over. Transfer to a plate and set aside.

- Add the remaining oil to the pan with the onion, pepper and garlic and cook until the onion is beginning to soften. Add the rice, wine, saffron and stock and bring to the boil. Cover and reduce to a simmer. Cook for 15 minutes or until the rice is nearly cooked. Stir once during the cooking period.

- Add the browned chorizo and chicken and cook until the chicken is cooked through — this should take no more than 5-6 minutes. Add the seafood and the lemon juice and cook for a further 2 minutes, or until the seafood is cooked through.

- Season, sprinkle with parsley and serve hot.

- **2, 3 and 4 Oven Aga,** cook rice in the Simmering Oven for 15 minutes. Add remaining ingredients, cover and place into the Simmering Oven until the prawns are cooked.

- **Rayburn,** cook rice in the Main Oven with the Thermodial reading Simmer for 15 minutes. Add remaining ingredients, cover and place back into the Main Oven until the prawns are cooked.

Variations

Vegetarian paella *Replace chicken with roasted butternut squash pieces.*

James says...

Saffron has a distinctive taste and flavour, but it's expensive. Why not replace the saffron with $1/2$ tbsp turmeric? Not only is it cheaper, but it makes the rice nice and golden too. Frozen sea food is generally cheaper than fresh.

chinese lamb chops.

An alternative way to cook chops.

150g fresh breadcrumbs   1 egg, beaten
1 tbsp Chinese five spice powder   8 lamb chops

Here's how to make it...

- Preheat the grill to a medium setting.
- Mix breadcrumbs and five spice powder together and add beaten egg. Mix through to bind. Make into 8 balls.
- Set a ball of breadcrumb mix onto each chop and press down well.
- Cook under the grill for 10 minutes.
- 2, 3 and 4 Oven Aga, cook on the 1st set of runners in the Roasting Oven for 10 minutes.
- Rayburn, cook on the 1st set of runners in the Main Oven with the Thermodial reading Roast.

Serve with...Vegetable stir fry or vegetable rice.

Variations

Chinese pork chops *Replace lamb chops with pork.*

James says...

Chinese five spice powder is commonly available in supermarkets and is a mix of a dried bud of the cassia flower, star anise, anise, ginger and cloves to give a sweet, sour, bitter and salty flavour.

macaroni cheese.

I never understood why this is such an old Scottish dish?

250g macaroni	600ml milk
40g butter	250g grated cheddar
40g plain flour	50g grated Parmesan

Here's how to make it...

- Preheat the grill to a high setting. Grease a deep sided oven proof dish.
- Cook the macaroni according to the pack instructions, drain and set aside.
- Place the butter, flour and milk into a pan and gently bring to the boil whisking continuously.
- Place the macaroni into the greased dish and pour the sauce over the top. Sprinkle with both cheeses and grill for 5–10 minutes until golden brown.
- **2, 3 and 4 Oven Aga,** cook on the 1st set of runners in the Roasting Oven for 5–10 minutes.
- **Rayburn,** cook on the 1st set of runners in the Main Oven with the Thermodial reading Roast.

Serve with... Green salad and fresh crusty bread.

Variations

Yellow and orange macaroni cheese *Replace cheddar with Red Leicester cheese.*

James says...

In this recipe I've used an all-in-one sauce instead of a roux.

lancashire hotpot.

Many variations of this dish exist, but none are as good as 'Betty's hotpot' from the Rovers Return on Coronation Street.

175g lambs kidneys, white core removed, skinned and halved
900g potatoes, thinly sliced
3 tbsp vegetable oil
8 lamb chops
3 leeks, sliced
2 carrots, peeled and thickly sliced

1 tbsp fresh chopped thyme or ½ tbsp dried thyme
Salt and freshly ground black pepper
600ml lamb stock
1 tbsp Worcestershire sauce
25g butter, melted

Here's how to make it...

- Preheat oven to 170°C (150°C if using a fan oven) or Gas Mark 3.
- Heat the oil in a frying pan and brown the chops on each side. Set aside.
- Using a large casserole dish, layer the meats, leeks, carrots and potatoes, seasoning and sprinkling with thyme between each layer. Finish with a layer of potato.
- Mix the stock and Worcestershire sauce together and pour over. Brush top of potatoes with melted butter.
- Cover and cook for 2 hours and then uncover and cook for 30 minutes to brown the potatoes.
- **2, 3 and 4 Oven Aga,** cook in the Simmering Oven for 2 hours, then uncover and cook on the 4th set of runners in the Roasting Oven for 30 minutes.
- **Rayburn,** cook on the 4th set of runners in the Main Oven with the Thermodial reading Simmer and then increase the temperature for the last 30 minutes so the Thermodial reads Roast.

Serve with... Seasonal vegetables.

Variations

Orange and date Lancashire hotpot *Add finely grated zest of 1 orange and 50g chopped dates.*

James says...

This is one of those recipes that tastes 100 times better if you make it with proper lamb stock, rather than using a stock cube.

chicken tagine.

In Morocco a tagine is both the name of the dish and the cooking vessel. The cooking vessel is conical in shape so any evaporation condenses and falls back onto the food, keeping the moisture in.

1kg chicken breast, cut
into bite-sized pieces
2 tsp ground ginger
2 tsp ground coriander
2 tsp turmeric
5 tbsp olive oil
Salt and freshly ground
black pepper
1 clove garlic, crushed

1 tbsp plain flour
4 shallots, peeled
1 tbsp tomato puree
450ml chicken stock
2 tbsp fresh chopped coriander
1 bay leaf
1 cinnamon stick
75g stoned dates
1 tbsp runny honey

Here's how to make it...

- Preheat oven to 180°C (160°C if using a fan oven) or Gas Mark 4.
- Place chicken in a bowl with the ginger, ground coriander, turmeric and 1 tbsp oil. Season, cover and leave to marinate overnight in the fridge.
- Heat 1 tbsp oil in a heavy-based casserole and brown the chicken in batches. Add the garlic and cook for 1 minute.
- Stir in flour, tomato puree, shallots, stock, herbs and cinnamon. Bring to the boil and cover. Cook for 1¼ hours.
- Discard bay leaf and cinnamon, add the dates and honey and return to oven for 15 minutes.
- **2, 3 and 4 Oven Aga**, cook in the Simmering Oven for 1¼ hours.
- **Rayburn**, cook in the Lower Oven with the Thermodial reading Roast or on the 4th set of runners in the Main Oven with the Thermodial reading Simmer for 1¼ hours.

Serve with... Couscous.

Variations

Lamb tagine *Substitute chicken for lamb.*
....
Beef tagine *Substitute chicken for beef.*
....

James says...

You can replace the turmeric for saffron. To use saffron, set it in a small cup of boiling water to infuse for a few minutes before cooking.

turkish kebabs. pork spare ribs. lemon garlic chicken. stir-fry chicken with bok choi. asian chicken and spinach curry. pork schnitzel. mushroom stroganoff. baked honey pork fillets. pork with mustard and apple. beef olives with thyme and juniper. irish stew. chicken with lemon wedges and thyme. moroccan lamb and couscous. lasagne with a ton of basil. chilli con carne. moussaka. chicken and mushroom pie. steak and ale pie. tagliatelle and meat balls. devilled chicken supremes. prawn, orange and ginger stir-fry. coq au vin. simple fish pie. chicken á la king. pancetta, pork and pea risotto. venison casserole. chicken fajitas. stuffed bacon rolls. chicken casserole. spaghetti carbonara. coley and lemongrass with a parsley sauce. braised lamb shanks in red wine and balsamic. sweet and sour pork. beef curry. kedgeree. penne arrabiata. sole florentine. jambalaya. bœuf bourguignon. teriyaki beef stir-fry. carbonade de bœuf. rich braised beef with herb dumplings. thai chicken curry. beef goulash. steak and kidney pie. paella. chinese lamb chops. macaroni cheese. lancashire hotpot. chicken tagine.

index of recipes.

asian chicken and spinach curry   16
asian chicken and watercress curry   17
asian almond chicken and spinach curry   17

baked honey pork fillets   22
baked honey chicken fillets   23
baked honey butternut squash   23

beef goulash   78

beef olives with thyme and juniper   26
beef olives with parsley and breadcrumbs   27

beef somerset   69

bœuf bourguignon   68

braised lamb shanks in red wine and balsamic   58
braised lamb shanks with parsnips   59

carbonade de bœuf   72
rich carbonade de bœuf   72

chicken á la king   49
smokey chicken á la king   49

chicken and mushroom pie   40
chicken and wild mushroom pie   41

chicken casserole   55
chicken and apricot casserole   55

chicken fajitas   43
prawn fajitas   43
steak fajitas   43

chicken goulash   79

chicken schnitzel   19
turkey schnitzel   19
pork schnitzel   18

chicken tagine   88
beef tagine   89
lamb tagine   89

chicken with lemon wedges and thyme   30
sticky chicken with lemon wedges and thyme   31

chilli con carne   36
mushroom chilli con carne   37
vegetable chilli   37

chinese lamb chops   84
chinese pork chops   84

coley and lemongrass with a parsley sauce   73
cod and lemongrass with a parsley sauce   73

coq au vin 47

curry 57
   beef curry 57
   chicken curry 57
   pork curry 57

devilled chicken supremes 45
   devilled pork sausages 45
   devilled pork chops 45

irish stew 28
   herb irish stew 29

jambalaya 66

kedgeree 62
   pesto kedgeree 63
   smoked trout kedgeree 63

lancashire hotpot 86
   orange and date lancashire hotpot 87

lasagne with a ton of basil 34
   bacon and goats cheese lasagne 35
   vegetable lasagne 35

lemon garlic chicken 13
   orange garlic chicken 13

macaroni cheese 85
   yellow and orange macaroni cheese 85

moroccan lamb and cous cous 32
   moroccan lamb and mint couscous 33

moussaka 38
   spicy moussaka 39

mushroom stroganoff 20
   beef stroganoff 21
   pork stroganoff 21
   chicken stroganoff 21
   turkey stroganoff 21

penne arrabiata 64
   spicy salami arrabiata 64

pork with mustard and apple 24

pork schnitzel 18
   chicken schnitzel 19
   turkey schnitzel 19

pork spare ribs 12
   curry spare ribs 12
   honey and sesame seed spare ribs 12
   spicy marmalade spare ribs 12

prawn, orange and ginger stir-fry — 46
chicken, orange and ginger stir-fry — 46
pork, orange and ginger stir-fry — 46

pancetta, pork and pea risotto — 50
porcini, pork and pea risotto — 51

rich braised beef with herb dumplings — 74
rich braised beef with herb and mustard dumplings — 75
rich braised venison with herb dumplings — 75

simple fish pie — 48
russian fish pie — 48

sole florentine — 65

spaghetti carbonara — 56
prawn spaghetti carbonara — 56

steak and ale pie — 42
steak and Guinness pie — 42

steak and kidney pie — 80
rich steak and kidney pie — 81

stir-fry chicken with bok choy — 14
stir-fry beef with bok choy — 15
stir-fry pork with bok choy — 15

stuffed bacon rolls — 54
apple and stilton bacon rolls — 54
apricot and walnut bacon rolls — 54

sweet and sour pork — 60
sweet and sour chicken — 61

tagliatelle and meat balls — 44
tagliatelle with pork and coriander meatballs — 44

teriyaki beef stir-fry — 70
teriyaki chicken stir-fry — 71
teriyaki pork stir-fry — 71
teriyaki salmon stir-fry — 71

thai chicken curry — 76
nutty thai curry — 77
thai beef curry — 77
thai fish curry — 77

turkish kebabs — 10
chinese five spice chicken kebabs — 10
greek souvlaki kebabs — 10
satay kebabs — 10

venison casserole — 52
venison and walnut casserole — 53

Other books by James

2008 Gourmand winner
- UK's Best Cookbook

mix.

mix. is a terrifically comprehensive guide
to basic proportions in cookery, giving the
quantities needed for simple, everyday
family food. Containing over 170 recipes,
from how to make a white sauce to how to
prepare pastry, this is an essential cookery
book you will turn to again and again.